My Guyana
Jungle Adventures

Lisbeth Cameron

Front cover photograph: Lisbeth with her talking Amazon parrott called Roger Varu, which means 'Older Brother' in Akawaio Amerindian language

First published in 2019 by Hawkes Design & Publishing Ltd.

ISBN: 978-1-9998335-6-5

"*To travel is to live*".

Hans Christian Andersen

Acknowledgements.

Thanks go to my niece, Sille, who gave me many good ideas and to my writing teacher, Linda Dawe, who guided and inspired me, plus Pat Abercromby, who after having published her own first book, spent a long time editing my text. Last but not least, a special thanks to my patient husband, Nick, who prepared the photos and helped me with all my IT questions.

Contents

Prologue

Was this a dream? I was living under a tarpaulin in a bush camp in the middle of the jungles of Guyana. Yet it was only a little more than a year since I had left cosy Denmark to train in England to be a midwife. Well this was no dream and the explanation was simple. I was newly married and as both of us wanted to travel, my English geologist husband, Nick, had arranged to be seconded from the Ministry of Housing Government department in London, (which does not exist anymore) to Guyana, where he would be working for the Guyanese Geological Survey. And the appointment began just a month after we were married.

I had absolutely no idea of what I let myself in for, but my time in Guyana's jungle would prove to be the most exciting thing I had ever done. There was so much to absorb from what proved to be a most civilised and carefully organised way of living far within the all encompassing wilds of the jungle.

Jungle view.

Guyana is a country located on the northern mainland of South America, neighbouring Brasil to its south, Suriname to the east, Venezuela to the west and the great Atlantic Ocean to the north. By many, it is considered to be part of the Caribbean due to its strong cultural and historical ties with that area. Guyana became independent in 1966 and changed its name from British Guiana to Guyana (pronounced without the "e" sound). Many British people are not aware of this change and the old pronunciation can still be heard, to the consternation of the Guyanese.

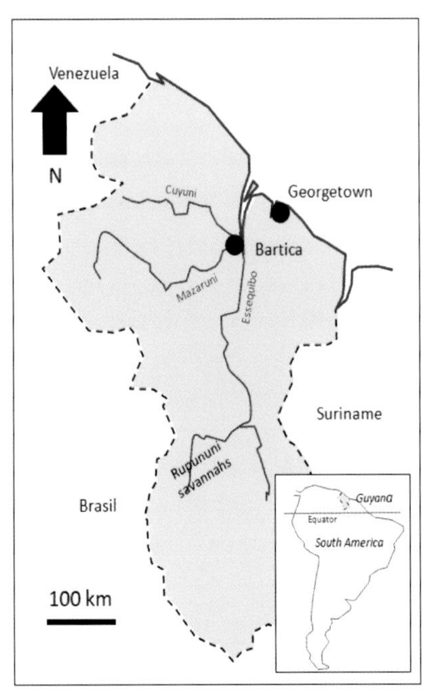

Map of Guyana.

We lived in Guyana from 1969 to 1973, though part of that time was spent working in Belém (Brasil, that is another story). During our time in Guyana, I spent seven months in the bush as it is often called. My strongest reminiscences are of waking up every day in a hammock, listening to the noises of the surrounding jungle - the birds, monkeys, distant large animals and the buzzing insects. My memories are of the daily routine of camp life and the various things that happened to us. Time was spent in a very simple, but highly organised way. I always felt totally safe: it seemed that if you respect nature, nature will look after you.

Untouched jungle

At the time we arrived in Guyana, expeditions to map the geology of the country and investigate its mineral resources were the everyday work of the Geological Survey. This meant most of my husband's work was in the bush away from the capital Georgetown.

In Guyana at the time and still today, most of the population live along the northern coast by the Atlantic Ocean or on the banks of the multiple rivers which criss-cross the country. Going further south the savannas cover huge areas of the Rupununi region, where many of the Amerindians live and where there are large cattle ranches. To the south, the jungle returns to link up with the Amazon jungle of Brasil. The high mountains in the north west against the border of Venezuela were described in the "Lost World" by Conan Doyle.

Guyana's population consists mainly of Africans and Indians plus the Amerindians. The first two arrived in Guyana to work in the sugar cane fields. They remain proud of their cultures, mixtures of which make up and define Guyana today. Portuguese, Chinese and Europeans also settled in the country.

I am forever grateful to the team of men from the Georgetown area and the inland Amerindian villages, along the rivers Mazaruni, Essequibo and Cayuni, who made our way of life possible through the use of their knowledge of the rivers, creeks and the resources of the jungle. They guided and took care of us, in addition to performing the skilled work required for expeditions.

Though one often reads about horrific jungle experiences, for example people lost in the jungle or suffering from attacks by big cats, small red ants and giant snakes, plus leeches. Also vividly described are jungle yaws, sores and bites that will not heel. We never experienced anything like this. The list of possible dangers is long, but due to our experienced team, we were and always felt safe.

All the things I am about to describe are true, though for continuity they are not necessarily placed in their correct order of events. In some cases, I may have remembered names incorrectly.

1. The adventures begin.

After locking our first floor government flat in New Market Street in Georgetown, we were driven, together with our supplies, by Land Rover the short distance across Georgetown to the *stelling* (quay). Here everyone collected to join the steamer that would take us to the mouth of the Demerara river, then briefly out to sea through the brown, Amazon silt stained waters of the Atlantic (most Guyanese have never seen blue sea and believe this is the sea's natural colour) before turning into the broad Essequibo and heading down past islands to the small, but ever busy town of Bartica.

The steamer stopped at stations on the way, loading on or off people, wares and animals. It was most enjoyable just to sit and see the selling of goods on the quayside amidst all the hustle and bustle of the ship.

Bustling activity at Fort Island stelling on the mouth of the Essequibo River.

Bartica town was built at the junction of the Essequibo, Mazaruni and Cuyuni rivers as a trading post and was the starting point of the only way to travel inland into the jungle at that time. The Geological Survey had an office, storage base, known as a *godown*, and a boat house in the middle of the town next to the ferry terminal and which was efficiently run by Mr. Ragnaught. Once all our supplies were transferred from the storage and ready for loading on to our boat for the next morning, we left to walk the short distance to Mrs Ghani's Karia Hotel to spend the night and enjoy her cooking. The streets around the harbour were busy and congested with people and goods to buy and sell and we needed to carefully thread our way through the market crowds, avoiding at the same time, wandering donkeys, cows and puddles to finally reach the calm coolness of our hotel, a comfortable old wooden house which stood on stilts high enough to keep it dry when there were floods.

The Survey's boat house at Bartica.

Bartica from Karia Hotel, where we stayed before continuing into the bush.
The Essequibo River is in the background.

First Avenue Bartica.

On the way we passed the school and the small hospital where I was able to work when I did not accompany Nick up river. There the staff coped with every eventuality that could happen in a frontier town. Occasionally the pharmacist had to manage when a doctor was not available.

A typical Bartica house. Many of these fine old houses no longer exist.

During the night in the Karia hotel I was woken by the scraping noise of one of my shoes being dragged further under the bed, but as soon I looked under the bed to find the cause the noise stopped. I tried to be quick each time it happened, but never managed to see anything, even when leaning far over the side of the bed with a torch in my hand. In the morning I found the back of my shoe had been eaten away: it must have been a lovely snack for a little mouse or maybe perhaps something bigger. Later I also realised that a piece of cake left over for a morning snack, had vanished, even though it was safely placed on top of a wardrobe. Little did I know then, that from now on my daily life would need to be adapted to the multiple challenges I was to encounter from the many wiles of nature and its creatures. Much later I would look back and miss the exciting days of sharing my bedroom with a mouse.

The next morning everything was ready and packed into the boat. After extracting some of the men from the bars and their debts paid for, we were ready to set off. Our boat or *bateau* was flat bottomed and designed to be, when necessary, pulled through the sides of rapids or when there were floods to "run" them. It was commanded by a captain and driven by two old, but easy to maintain Archimedes outboard engines. It contained all the stores, trunks and tools for the forthcoming work, plus space for everyone and the vital tarpaulin to cover camps and everything when, as they would on most days, the rains came.

Little did I know how rapidly and dangerously rivers could change.

2. Into the unknown

It was quickly getting darker. The only sound was the water hitting the boat and the noise of the engines as it moved slowly along the river. The banks were covered by trees and as the daylight was drawing in, the vegetation stood like a dark wall, impenetrable on both sides.

Travelling to camp. Walter Rekha our camp attendant (on the right), Rodney, Eastwick, Alec, Lawrence and Captain Mackay.

I had never been anywhere like this before. I did not know what would happen, where we were going or in what conditions we might find shelter later on. The smells were different. Overriding was dampness and the sharp, acid smell of rotten leaves, but it was not unpleasant. Before darkness, I had noticed that the water on the river was clear, but brown in colour. I could see the bottom, see the branches and the vegetation in the water, but the brownness could be lighter or darker as the boat moved along the river.

The side of the boat was close to the water. Just by letting my hand hang out over the boat, I could touch the cool water. The motor, with their "tuck-tuck-tucks" melted into the sound of the small waves hitting the sides of the boat. There were fifteen or so men sitting around me on the sides of the boat, each in their own thoughts, not giving me or anyone else attention.

We were completely surrounded by darkness on both sides, but when looking up the sky appeared lighter between the trees, forming a long line of deep blue colour interspersed by blinking stars between the overhanging trees. In spite of not having any kind of light on the river, this line of light was the captain's only guidance for navigation. After years of travelling this river he knew every inch of the way.

Occasionally a startled bird would make a cry of alarm when flapping away or a bigger animal at ground level would be disturbed, making a disgruntled noise followed by the rustlings of leaves as it disappeared into the darkness. These were noises I had never heard before and of things so far, completely unknown to me.

Now when the sun had gone down I could feel the cooling of the air. During the day, one could easily be soaked in the hot sun, already at 10 o'clock in the morning my waistline would be visibly wet, but now a cardigan would have been appreciated.

More jungle. Animals were all but invisible to me - the man standing nearby can barely be seen.

3. The camp site

Having travelled beneath thick canopies of trees for so long in the dark, it was startling to be woken from my far away thoughts to suddenly become aware that there was a clearance ahead on the river bank. This was the camp site. Men had gone ahead to prepare everything for our arrival. Individual tents had been built from the felled trees for cooking, sleeping and work. Welcoming lights shone. I learned later that the biggest danger in the jungle is from large nuts, ferns or branches falling from the trees above us, during storms or even in the quiet of night, which means a campsite must never be covered by trees. In our case, the camp site had been carefully checked for such dangers and found to be safe.

Even more jungle.

On closer look, each camp (the name also given to individual tents) was constructed using four big, sturdy poles, one in each corner all covered by a tarpaulin which was supported by a lengthwise roof or ridge pole. That was to be our home for the next couple of months; it was two metres wide and three metres long. It was high enough to be able to stand up inside. We had cover from the rain, but no privacy, since walls were not part of the design. I will come back to what might happen in a camp with no walls.

Clearing the bush for a camp site.

The completed camp.

Camp life.

A ditch had been dug around the circumference of the camp to drain away rainwater falling onto the tarpaulin or tarps, as they were known, and aiding the rain flooding the ground to soak into the earth and not enter the camp. Since tropical rain would hit the tarpaulin with great force and in huge volumes, this ditch proved to be essential in keeping us dry inside. It was yet another example of the bush skills our crew brought with them. In addition, there was tarpaulin on the floor: a rather civilised means of keeping things clean and dry. Several, short sticks were stuck into the ground just inside the tent. The explanation for their presence was simple. Shoes and boots should be kept upside down so that no creepy-crawlies, such as scorpions, would be tempted to go inside for shelter and bite the owner when they were put on again. Furthermore, one should always stamp on the shoe or boot before wearing it; to be double sure that nothing had taken occupancy inside. At one end of the tent more sticks were stuck into the ground. Here strung across them were shelves made of sticks bound together, for placing belongings such as clothes and books. Very civilized indeed. A real touch of home.

Next to our tent was our camp attendant's camp and kitchen. He was there to cook our food, and to keep everything clean and tidy and sometimes also helped with the expedition's work. First we had Harold Rekka and later his son, Walter.

Our camp with hammocks and the luxury bookshelf.

Hammocks were quickly strung up and we could not wait to get to sleep. Have you ever tried sleeping in a hammock? The obvious way is to simply lie along the length of the hammock. A far better way is to stretch out across the diagonal, for example from the upper left corner to the lower right corner. This way keeps the back straight and we soon found this position was incredibly comfortable.

But there was another complication to surmount before we could climb in and sleep. Due to the danger of insect and rabid bat bites, the hammocks had to be inserted into a hammock mosquito net. This horrible, but vital item is best described as a sausage skin around a sausage. First we had to crawl in through a tiny tunnel at the side of the mosquito net and then find the hammock and eventually stretch it out with our feet. This was not easy to do. After having spent half an hour falling out and landing on the ground or finding ourselves in the most ridiculous positions, we eventually managed to settle down for our first night. We slowly became more proficient with this procedure, without letting any mosquitoes in, which is important. We also learned to keep our hands and feet away from the net, since rabid bats like to bite into fingers or any available toes.

The tropical night beneath trees is pitch black with only light glimmers coming from the other camps. The sounds of strange insects in the quiet night and the flicker of the moon between the trees were my last impressions of my first day before falling soundly asleep.

A camp site by the river.

4. Camp Life

The first thing I saw the next morning on awakening was a snake just above my head. It was lying along the long roof pole and had placed itself very comfortably with its body curled in elegant coils along the length of the pole. My first thought was to move as slowly as possible out of the way. Not easy considering that I had to crawl out through the narrow entry hole of the mosquito net without setting the hammock into a swinging movement and so disturbing the snake. But the snake did not move, just lying in a relaxed position criss-crossing the pole. I noticed then it would have been difficult to see if it had been on the ground, as it skin was greyish and brownish in colour. Luckily then that it was up there and not down on the ground.

Calling out I got the attention of one of the men. He put his head in and laughed. He assured me that I was very lucky to have this particular snake in residence since it survives by eating other snakes. Apparently many kinds of snakes in South America prey on other snakes. Feeling much better after I knew that it was not interested in me, I could start my day in this exciting new world.

Kitchen activities with Gilbert.

This was just the first of many times I had to rely on the men for safety and guidance. Most were not city dwellers, but bush people who knew the jungle like the backs of their hands. For example, they knew the name of every single tree, even it was a sapling or fully grown with its crown invisible from the ground. They knew which tree to cut out for paddles, firewood or handles for tools, as well as which wood to use for making ornaments.

In this part of Guyana, I later found out, there are over three hundred different species of trees. Especially valuable for timber is the Green Heart. Though the wood and bark are pleasantly scented, I was told that if I was unfortunate enough to get a splinter from this tree that it would probably become poisonous. These trees are slow growing and their timber is in danger of being over exploited. Another tree was Purple Heart, good for carving, with its outer white and purple inner wood. We were given a beautiful Amerindian head carved from this wood.

One day we ran out of lavatory paper. I decided to collect leaves instead and I quickly found some really big ones which looked perfect. As I went around collecting the leaves, someone asked me what I wanted to use them for. When he realised, he said I should not touch them at all since they produce a most annoying itch and so they did. Fortunately, I had only touched the leaves with my left hand and just had to suffer until the itch disappeared. It was unthinkably what could have happened to my more delicate parts?

When the men returned home to the camp, after a day's work, they would collect vines as they walked. In the evening, under the bright light from kerosene burning Tilley lamps, they would stain the vines with colours extracted from flowers and roots. Then they would plait the vines into very beautiful baskets (some we still have on display at home) or fans for flaming up the cooking fires. They also made for work *warishees*, a carrying frame hung on the back from the shoulders with a broad strap around the forehead for further support. It was used for transporting loads of up to sixty plus kilos through the bush. This was the way they carried bush meat home when they went out hunting for the camp.

We were taught to live with snakes. Of course we had to take certain precautions. I have already mentioned that shoes and boots were placed upside down on sticks for safety so not to tempt any creatures of the jungle, to think that here was a nice, cosy corner to spend time. In addition, if we were late after our evening bath in the river, walking home at dusk, we needed to make as much noise as possible. The result was that we stamped the ground with every step to warn snakes and any other unwelcome inhabitants that we were approaching.

Me and Nick with warishees made by Mr Smithies who is standing next to Nick.

Staining vines to be used for making coloured baskets, examples of which are shown in the next picture.

Finished products made by Joe and Milton.
Roger Varu, our parrot, which accompanied us into the bush and who inevitably found himself in my pictures. Here he is showing off by hanging upside down below Milton's basket. The makers are Wapishanas from Sand Creek in the southern savannahs.

An access line cut through the jungle.

When the men were working, they necessarily walked in a line through the jungle along paths cut through the vegetation with their cutlasses. They knew that it was always the third man who would get bitten by an angry snake. The first man would disturb the snake, the second would annoy it and the third would be bitten.

At night the camp took on a cosy look from the light of the kerosene lamps and the fires. The men relaxed by washing, reading or playing games like cards or "cracking" dominoes. I was just passing by a tent once, when a knife came flying by, hitting the ground just in front of me. One of the Amerindians had, when playing cards, seen movements out of the corner of his eye and his knife hit a poisonous snake that I surely would have trod on. This is just yet another proof of the expertise of the Amerindians we lived with and their powers of observation and knowledge of the jungle environment. I remain grateful to his observation and accuracy with a knife. I never had any fear in camp: this incident just made me feel doubly safe.

Nathan and Stanford relaxing after work.

When drilling was taking place the men worked in shifts through the day. At night this was done using light from a generator.

Drilling for copper and gold at Groete Creek.
The wooden rack is for examining cored rock.

*

Groete Creek drillers between shifts.

Night drilling at Groete Creek.

5. Daily hygiene

After the men, including Nick, left camp at seven in the morning to start their daily activities, I could leave to enjoy a swim in a nearby creek. I found it reassuring that no one was about, maybe a camp attendant or if someone was unwell, resting in another camp. The creek was ten metres wide with a calm current running down the middle. The water was clear, but of the brown jungle colour provided by the tannin released by the rotting vegetation. Each side of the banks could be steep and covered with vegetation, but I had made my own easy to get up and down place. I always enjoyed this clean, in spite of the colour, fresh water.

As I was splashing around in the coolness of the creek water, a big Anaconda suddenly swam into view bending its body from side to side in the current as it approached. It passed me without taking any notice which was fortunate as an anaconda can quickly bite and curl its body around the victim, crushing the bones until "dinner" could be swallowed whole. Well not me that day. Maybe it had just eaten.

Swimming in brown creek water before I saw the Anaconda.

Going to the lavatory in camp with so many men present could have been a problem. Fortunately, such needs had already been planned for. A deep, square hole was dug some distance from the camp with the dug up earth left, with a shovel, in a big pile next to the hole. Two poles were put into the ground on each side of the hole with a third pole fixed by vines between them. This was the "seat" to rest against. A grab stick, sometimes known as a "straining stick", was placed in front of the hole to cling on to when sitting and so prevent falling backwards into the hole. After each visit, a shovel full of earth was thrown back to cover up the results. This prevented flies and any smell developing. When the hole was filled, another was dug a small distance away. Many such lavatories were dug around the circumference of the camp. Some people would call them “long drop”. Nick and I had our own "retreat".

Because I was present, the men kindly made a screen or wall next to our hole on the side, facing the camp. It was made of braided palm leaves and gave the only women in the camp considerable privacy.

Joe Emanuel has a haircut by Milton Roberts.

One evening after sunset I picked up my torch and wondered out to our "private place". I put the torch still lit on the ground and was “sitting” in my own thoughts when suddenly I noticed the shadow of a big "tiger" on the screen (big jungle cats, such as panthers, are colloquially called "tigers" in Guyana). I froze. I thought I would end my days as tiger food, but then I heard a small "meow". That was from my own cat, which I had brought with me from Georgetown, and which had followed me out of the camp. Much to my relief, I realised the torch light had projected an enlarged shadow of our cat onto the screen

On another night, I needed to go and thought I could just sit behind the nearest tree instead of walking all the way to the “place”. When I checked the ground to see if it was clear, the torch light revealed a grey spider the size of a big hand sitting on a tree root, with spikes on its legs. But what made me jump were two, one meter long antennae protruding from the spider’s head into the air. Later I found out that this particular spider was harmless and just likes to sit on tree roots as it was doing.

Thereafter, I was always aware that I was never truly alone in the bush, but always surrounded by the animal and the insect world. One day as I once again was splashing the water when washing clothes, I heard growling that to me sounded to be coming from a really big tiger. As usual I could not see anything, only thick bush. But something was nearby and let its displeasure known to me, just a short warning, no more thank goodness. I must admit I tried to wash in other creeks thereafter.

Washing day.

Where's my soap gone?

Washing was no problem as there were plenty of rivers and smaller creeks: you could say we had "installed running water". However, we were camped close to the Equator in jungle which meant the humidity was always near 100%. In that environment, it took a long time to dry those easily washed clothes. Even when finding a spot of direct sunshine, the clothes took ages to dry. The situation during the rainy season was impossible. I would hang the clothes out and ten minutes later I would hear, what we knew as the "rain bird" calling. It had a distinct call with a high pitch, warning the surroundings that in five minutes time the rains would come. Its sound could be heard clearly under the canopy of trees, often as an echo. And the bird was always right: I would desperately run around taking everything under cover.

Even when the rain bird was not warning me, I could hear the rain hitting the leaves from far away. The noise came closer and closer. Suddenly it would hit you like a thick, moving curtain, followed by thunder. After five minutes it stopped and I would carry all the laundry out again. Then the bird would warn me again. This activity would in the rainy season take place many times during the day. In spite of all my efforts, it could take three days to dry just a handkerchief.

In reality nothing much could dry and the result was that clothes would give off that peculiar sharp smell of the forest. We always smelled like that and after a short while we became used to it. However, it was all too obvious when on our return to our flat in Georgetown, we unpacked our gear and the whole flat soon smelt of acid, woody, musty jungle. A smell which forever will remind me of the jungle.

Across the bush on our way home to Georgetown.

6. Domesticated animals in the camp and other incidents

Because we were away from home for so long, it was difficult to leave our pets behind. I owned during my time in the camps two local cats, a green, Amazon talking parrot called “Roger Varu”, which in Carib Amerindian means "older brother", and a small, green and orange parakeet which was called Palakia. The birds came from Amerindian villages we visited. At the end of our time in Guyana we were able to return them to their original homes.

Palakia where she was happiest.

Having such incompatible pets was generally considered to be impossible, but I can only say that in my experience it all worked out most amenably. I would introduce the cat and bird to each other by putting beak to nose and hitting the cat once. After this introduction the cats, knew their place, but the parrots, unfortunately, would take advantage of the situation and tease the cats. I could watch the parrot going up to the cat in the most provocative way, perhaps biting its tail, and then looking to me as if it was asking for permission or just checking out its degree of protection. However, I never lost a bird to the cats.

When travelling into the bush, I had my two cats in my handbag and two parrots in a cage made of rattan or vines cut from the bush. Unfortunately, the birds often bit their way out of the cage and preferred to sit on my shoulder or on top of my head when travelling. I was forever repairing the basket.

Palakia had escaped again from her basket and sat as usual on my head as we travelled down the river

The men told me on several occasions that they were relieved it was cats I had brought into the bush and not dogs. They believed that dogs were considered by tigers to have a sweet taste, but they were not interested in cats, maybe because of their close relationship. They told me that even if I slept with a dog in my arms, the tiger would take the dog without me noticing anything. I was told many strange stories and in our situation surrounded by trees, rivers and strange noises, especially to me, maybe there was some truth in the stories?

The birds had a lovely time in the bush. Every morning they would climb up into the trees and enjoy eating the fruits and flowers at the crown of the trees. We could not see the flowers high up, we only saw the petals lying on the ground. The birds might come down at lunchtime when we were eating around a collapsible table in the tent. They would walk across the ground from their tree and climb up to the table top to get at the food on the plates.

Palakia joining me at lunch.

I had taken the precaution to cut one wing slightly so they would fall gently to the ground if they fell, which they never did, but that prevented them from taking off and disappearing.

7. Love and its hazards

During the travel with the steamer from Georgetown to reach Bartica some big crates full of yellow chicks were taken on board. The men bought some, taking them in their pockets all the way to camp, hoping to make an addition to their bush diet. The chickens quickly got used to the camp walking around all day pecking at whatever they could find to eat. There were plenty of insects for them, plus spilt things such as rice grains.

The chicks rapidly grew and soon we had eight hens walking around the camp. Palakia, the parakeet, was much taken with a particular hen and followed her around all day, unreciprocated in her love. We had much amusement watching the small bird trying to get the attention of a completely uninterested hen. The large size of the hen created many problems for the little parakeet. Sometimes the hen would happen to tread on Palakia, who desperately tried to get away if its beak became trapped under the heavy hen's foot.

I liked my shelves of sticks in the camp to put my things on; it gave me a feeling of civilisation in the middle of the bush. I could keep my books and alarm clock there. Unfortunately the chickens loved to sit on my "bookshelves". I did not appreciate that, since they would make droppings over everything. I spent considerable time shushing them out and cleaning up after them.

One of the provisions we took into the bush was a big barrel of salted pork. The parakeet soon found the barrel and during the day we would hear squawking from the complaining bird as the camp attendant threw it out and put the lid on.

Occasionally the camp would get important visitors from Georgetown. When one VIP was giving a talk standing in the opening of a camp, all attention was focused not on him, but instead on a small inquisitive parakeet hanging by one leg from the roof of the camp trying to land on his head. We had to confess later that the parakeet had, perhaps deliberately, interfered with his presentation.

It was not surprising how well the two birds adapted to the jungle, but more amazing was to see how well two domesticated cats took to their new surroundings. I often heard thumping noises in the night against the tarpaulin we had on the ground inside the camp. The next morning I found three mice tails on the ground. The cats had played with and eaten their catch as cats do.

They would go anywhere disappearing for hours. The men, who covered long distances every day, said they saw the cats hunting far away. But they would come back every night to stay in the camp. No doubt cats have developed more attachment than we give them credit for.

8. Animals and creepy crawlies

One of the most beautiful sights in the jungle is a slightly metallic and shimmering looking, deep blue, large butterfly, gracefully floating by, called a Morpho. It would be seen in sunny clearings where they sat warming themselves. The wing span can be as big as a human hand. Because of its beauty, it is often known to people who never have been to the jungle. I later read that their blue colour is not caused by pigmentation, but is a phenomenon in which hue changes according to the angle of the light that hits the wings.

I thought it was only the Morpho that was so brightly blue coloured. But I soon knew differently. This happened when I was surprised one day getting out of the river and trying to get up a steep bank, when suddenly a spider appeared in front of me, but this time quite close to my face. It had a circumference the size of my palm and had the same most unusual, blue, shiny colour of the better known butterfly. I froze and called for help. It was not the size of the spider that alarmed me, but what was it capable of doing when I was trapped on a steep bank? Some can jump, others spit and of course they might also be able to bite. Our camp attendant, on seeing it, vanished in the opposite direction. Nick came with a long oar and moved the creature away. I felt sorry for this beautiful spider, but better safe than sorry.

I have also seen blue frogs, covered with the same blue-metallic colour. Nature is beautiful and forever fascinating. I learned many years later from a David Attenborough TV programme that bright coloured frogs can be toxic if touched.

One of the most interesting creatures and often not thought of as jungle inhabitants are ants. They were everywhere, as always busy, living in their different ways. They came in many sizes and colours. The smallest was a minute red ant called a “fire ant”, maybe because of their red colour, but more likely because of their strong bite. They were absolutely tiny, but if you happened to stand in their way, a bite between the toes would be most painful and result in the whole foot swelling up for several days. Looking at the reaction of my foot, it is difficult to understand the strong reaction of my body to a bite from something so small.

My favourite ant was the leaf cutting ant or *Cushi* as they are known locally. I spent many entertaining and most humorous hours watching them. They would cut up leaves on a tree and carry them into their colony. They knew that the trees they attacked could die and they would never cut leaves from the tree below which, they had made their nests. The result was that they often had a long distance to carry the pieces of leaves. The ants do not eat the leaves, but survive by eating a fungus which grows on the leaves.

All this is painstaking work for an ant. It is quite a task to move along the rough ground, climb into a tall tree, cut the leaf into small bits the size of a 5p coin, but still often bigger than themselves, and carry it all the way back to their nest in the ground. Several ants might assist another and often a smaller ant would sit on top of a piece of leaf being carried away. This was hilarious since the ant on top did not help in carrying, but was carried by the others. I suppose the small ant was an apprentice and learning, but it must have found just clinging on to a piece of irregularly moving leaf quite difficult.

Every camp had a provisions store. Here sacks of flour and rice, tins of margarine and bags of powdered egg were kept, together with the big barrels of salted pork. Early one morning it looked like it had started to snow in a long, neat line. Ants were emerging from the provision store with each ant carrying a grain of rice and disappearing under the roots of a huge tree at the edge of the camp. Help! Our valuable rice was being quickly carried away by the leaf cutting ants. It was fascinating to see, but rice was also our food, so this had to be stopped. This we did by moving the rice. We speculated as to why jungle ants liked rice. Some said that maybe the ants were feeding on some fungus which had developed on the surface of the rice. Maybe it was easier to raid a store than cut leaves high up trees.

If we wanted to keep some food in our own camp, we found that it would always attract ants of many kinds. Because it was a painful nuisance to have them crawling everywhere, we had to develop a strategy for keeping them out. We would hang the delicacy from a rope in the middle of the tent from the tarpaulin's roof pole. Problem solved? No such chance. Ants can crawl up tarpaulins, along the supporting pole, down the rope and enjoy a good bite. We had to think of something else.

In front of the kitchen tent with Walter.

The men advised us to put the four legs of our small collapsible table into tins filled with kerosene. This would prevent the ants getting up to the table top. Well it worked half the time. However, ants are ruthless, like soldiers at war. The first ants would drown as they crossed and the rest would just walk across on top of them. Some ants would get through, but fortunately in smaller numbers than before.

Another ant called a *Monari* was huge, over an inch long with claws in front of a big head. It was black with a narrow waist and smaller abdomen. Everyone showed respect to these ants. A man in the camp showed me a Monari which was hanging on the side of his knife blade after having clenched its jaws on it. The man cut the ant in half and could not even then pull the head off the blade. He told me if you get bitten by one of these ants that you will not sleep a whole night from the pain. Well worth knowing in the middle of the jungle.

As mentioned before we only had tarpaulin for the roof, but no sides. One morning we saw enormous paw marks from a tiger who took a trip through the camp. They were the size of a man's hand. The men said that the curious animal just wanted to see what we were up to. One day the story went around that one of the men resting in his hammock suddenly felt someone hitting his bottom under the hammock and just one second afterwards he got a second hit. It turned out that an Armadillo was running for its life followed closely by a bigger cat. That is the danger of having your hammock too close to the ground when animals can run through. Of course all kinds of animals would pass through the camp since it was us who were camped in their environment.

On another occasion during a wet night, someone felt something moving beside him. His first thought in his sleep was that it was a fallen stick, but then he realised sticks do not move and he was fully awake in an instance since the stick could only be a snake. And it was. It had come in for warmth by way of the ridge pole supporting his hammock.

We had a turtle wandering through and I tied it up to make a change of menu. The men said I should keep it upside down otherwise it would escape. I did that and was surprised to see how the turtle by stretching its head backwards had managed to turn itself around. The next morning it had escaped anyway. I was relieved. But later Walter (our capable camp attendant) cooked turtle soup using another turtle. This was indeed a bush delicacy but I only had a big foot, tough as leather.

A little mouse was once caught and put into a glass jar with holes in the lid for breathing. Whatever we gave the mouse, it would not eat so after several days I let it go. When I tipped it out of the jar, it just sat there on the ground without moving. Suddenly it must have realised that it was free and it shot off into the undergrowth. Poor thing, it was so frightened that it had not eaten for three days.

A bush piglet found in the jungle.

A sloth swimming across the Cuyuni.
It was coloured green by algae living on its fur.

I do not know if the rivers had alligators. But we had small land alligators, only a few feet long. They could be seen around, usually between the trees on the ground. We used to eat anything that moved, but I do not remember eating them, though I did try them when in Brasil.

After a heavy downpour, we were often surrounded by "rain ants". They can be seen both in tropical and temperate areas. When the queen wants to start a new colony, they develop wings and the whole nest swarms just after the rain has passed. All that can be seen soon afterwards are thousands of wings on the ground.

When sitting at evening time under the tarpaulin with the kerosene lamp lit, the light unfortunately would attract the insects. At one stage I heard an unusual flying noise and a most unusual insect happened to end up in my mug of tea. I can only describe it as a green, flying triangle. When I fished it out it continued to fly around. It had a very sharp green colour and a compact, triangular body, the size of a fly. I never saw it described in a book and it never appeared in my tea or otherwise again.

9. Medicine and misconceptions

When the men started out every morning to collect samples from the jungle or along the rivers, they all carried cutlasses. They were necessary for cutting lines or trails through the bush and to make short cuts back home under the trees to the camp. As they walked along, they would swing their cutlasses from side to side to cut the side branches for others to follow along behind them. In spite of constantly using these big knives when walking, no accidents took place, even when they were swinging them left right, left right throughout the day.

A giant silk cotton tree.

I found it very difficult to see where a trail had been cut and considered it easier to see where the leaves on the ground had been compressed by footprints. Or maybe that was my imagination because the men were laughing on the way back at my interpretation. I also imagined that I could hear the leaves on the ground rustle when a snake or other small animals passed by. This view was also discredited using all kinds of jokes, for example they teased me and said perhaps I was also able to smell the snakes on the ground!

Apart from joking about my ignorance, life was serious in the bush. We had a simple first aid kit, but it was a worry to think how we could cope with bigger accidents. It sometimes crossed my mind if anyone got appendicitis or likewise, how quickly we could get him in a tiny boat down the river. Several places had rapids or big boulders of rocks, which made it necessary to carry the boat past the obstruction. With a sick person in pain, it could take several days before we could get to the nearest, small hospital in Bartica. And there might be no doctor there at that time, just the very competent pharmacist.

Occasionally trips were made if anyone needed to attend their families in the outside world. One came back looking very smug having been to his dentist and now his mouth was glittering with two rows of golden teeth. He felt very special and no doubt others felt a little jealous. Unfortunately, after a week he began to have severe toothache. The result was an urgent back down the river trip to receive treatment for a severe infection. Not a good advertisement for that dentist. And he was no longer so smug when he returned and became the subject of banter from everyone.

This sort of thing can happen to anyone. Once we were on home leave, when I needed a filling in my front tooth. My family wanted me to have the best treatment and arranged for an appointment in Harley Street. When I entered the "clinic", I was shocked to see it was a sitting room with sofas and pot plants in the window. The lamp over me was covered in dust. I have plenty of dust at home, but I do not operate on bone in my sitting room. I wondered how clean the instruments on the side table were. I should have been sensible and jumped out, but one was well behaved in those days.

I later distinctly felt that it was infected and had pain the following week, but we were away again and now I suffered the consequences. I was now swelling up in the face and found it difficult to open my mouth for eating.

We were visiting an Amerindian village called Jawalla on the Mazaruni River where we had some friends. We were three days up the river and there were no boat available. I just had to bear it. Fortunately for me, the pain subsided after three days. I actually forgotten about this and three years later, when attending a routine appointment with my dentist (in Copenhagen) I was told I had an abscess right up into my nose. I considered myself lucky as it could have been worse.

One of the few times the first aid kit was used was when my husband felt it necessary to give a tetanus injection. In those days the vaccine was prepared on horse serum and it was good practice to ask if the person was allergic to horses. The immunisation was given and Nick did not think more of it. The next morning a delegation of eight men stood in front of the tent. They wanted to know why that question was asked. A long explanation followed. “Aha” they said as they thought that my husband was worried if the patient would kick him when giving the injection.

I noticed one day that one of the men was walking around with a nasty swollen eye which was completely closed. On examination, I found a boil just below the eye. Having cleaned it up, removing the green pus and applying a little antibiotic cream, I recommended rest, a remedy which quickly made him feel better again.

It was believed among the Guyanese that if they made tea of selected leaves and sometimes also roots, that it was a healthy thing to do. Colloquially it was called “bush tea”. They would even give it to their babies and children. After having stayed several months in the bush, the men wanted to be prepared to go home to their wives. They thought a good brew of tea made from selected roots would work wonders as a strong aphrodisiac. Sometime later we were very sorry to hear that ten or so had poisoned themselves and some could not be saved. It must have been town people; this would never have happened to Amerindians.

Once Nick had noticed that there was blood on his pillow every morning. I could not detect anything and asked for advice in the camp. Apparently it was a fly which has laid an egg under the skin in his scalp and he was now harbouring a growing worm. I was told to chew some tobacco and spit it out to cover where the worm was sitting. That was tried without any result. I could now see something going up and down in a small hole. The worm was breathing. I decided to suffocate the unwelcome visitor with Vaseline sealing it in with a plaster. Success. The next morning I pulled the plaster off with the worm stuck to it. It was a ten millimetres long (or about half an inch), white maggot with small brown hairs on it. It left a small hole in my husband's head which quickly healed up.

As mentioned before we always used mosquito nets around our hammocks. One particular reason for this was the danger of rabies transferred by infected bats. The vampire bat in South America gets infected by biting already infected bush or domesticated animals, but strangely enough it only transmits the rabies without becoming sick itself. At night time they would bite humans and in this way transmit the rabies. We were always advised not to let a toe or arm rest close to the net. It would be a worry if one woke up to find blood on the bedding in the morning. That would have required a journey to town for an antiserum injection. That did happen to another geologist.

A tense moment on the Cuyuni.
Captains Ferreira, Mosely and Mackay, King, Eastwick and Monyham.

10. Visitors and other diversions

My life was peaceful from waking up to falling asleep just listening to the unusual noises or just the complete quietness. Generally the men in the camp talked and made noises and unknown animals let themselves be heard.

We were isolated in spite of having radio contact with the office and everyone enjoyed visits from the outside world. Any visitors of course had to make the same journey up the river and most became, like me, enchanted by the forest. Others did not really enjoy their time in the "wild". The visitors were mainly geologists from the office who came to be updated on the progress of the field work. For us it meant we would have companions to catch up on gossip over an after dinner drink; mainly tea, coffee or sometimes ovaltine. There was nothing cosier than sitting around the kerosene lamp, talking, and surrounded by the sounds of the jungle or the falling rain.

One of the most fascinating visitors was a botanist, Adrian Thompson, who had been flying over the jungle and noticed a small lake on top of a mountain (actually just a hill) nearby and which was open to the sky. This he considered to be most unusual. We were contacted by him and he arranged to come and visit us. Fortunately, Nick was aware of the location of the lake so we all walked there through the bush until we found the lake and stood at the water's edge. The biologist wanted to explore further. It was decided that a raft should be made for this investigation. The three Amerindians who were with us immediately started felling trees to make a raft. Before beginning they would check how the vines were running from tree to tree. This must be done so not to pull more trees down than they required or cause accidents. Then, when the trees were free of vines, cutting could begin. Though ordinary axes were used they made short work of each tree. Each tree came down with a huge crash making the ground shake. The trees in this area were made of heavy wood, so heavy that it could not float as well as normal wood. The result was that the raft floated just half way beneath the surface of the water and the person on the raft would stand with their feet in water. The biologist was excited about going out on the lake and he discovered a little frog that had never been described before. He named the lake Yellow Frog Lake.

Mr Smithies steering the raft as we came back from the lake.

To walk around with Adrian was fascinating. He observed minute insects or smaller animals which I would never see. As we were walking along he suddenly said "Hold this bag for me". I was given a plastic bag and without thinking held it close to the ground. He had noticed a black scorpion, which was very difficult to see. No doubt they were everywhere, just not observed by me. As I held the plastic bag open, he manoeuvred the scorpion into the bag as it swung its tail with its sting across the body for defence and finally was coaxed inside. Afterwards he said that I might have been frightened holding the bag, but that never crossed my mind; I was fascinated to learn about these insects. It was a beautiful specimen, 4-5 cm long, shiny black with its tail perfectly curled across the body.

He was also well travelled and had spent much time in Guyana and other countries. One day he told us that he had taken some Amerindians in Brasil to Manaus as he wanted them to see the world outside the jungle. These men were dressed in loincloths, had body paint and feathers in their ears. They carried a bow and arrows over their shoulders. He took them to Manaus harbour to board a modern fishing boat. He showed them the bridge, the navigation instruments, the deck and the cabins. They followed him around without saying anything, just observing the surroundings. Standing on the deck, he asked them of their impressions. They just looked over the side of the boat and all they said was: "You will need a very long fishing line".

This story, in my opinion, just shows that we humans only understand the world to the limit of the knowledge gained from our own past experiences and cannot readily utilise new ideas and new ways of doing things. Nick later pointed out that, though they were attuned to the ways of the jungle, where we could not survive, they would soon be lost in our daily traffic, buildings or airports.

Another time a Guyanese geologist, Maurice, who was working with Nick in the office, came to join us in the bush. Our camp attendant, Walter, provided meat and rice, and we enjoyed an evening talking to our guest under the tree tops sitting at the entrance to our camp in the cool air. Maurice told us, when he was younger, that he was sent by the Guyanese Government to study in what was at that time East Germany. It was cold for someone brought up in the tropics and the food was not as plentiful as he was used to. A very rare delicacy was oranges which only occasionally were available there. But he decided, though he would like one, to let his host have them because he could get more than plenty on his return to Guyana.

We were once contacted through a friend by the Bishops' High School who wanted to educate their students about the jungle, as few Guyanese ever go there. We were able to arrange to give a class of school girls an opportunity to come and visit and experience camp life since we were camped not far from Bartica. After having seen the camp and learned about trees and what to do and not do in the bush, they returned to write up their project. As a farewell gift, they were presented with Nick's worm which I had just extracted from his head. Who knows what they did with it. Maybe it ended up being preserved and exhibited in the school, along with the other collections they made that day in the jungle?

Of course the men relaxed in the evenings telling each other of strange happenings. One of the most experienced and respected persons was Mr. Best. I never found out if this was his real name or just a nickname. His name was true to his character anyway. He was a tall, thin African who could put his hand to anything. He was clever at repairing tools and vehicles, and his knowledge of the jungle was appreciated by everyone. He could cut up wild animals, tell stories and was the most trustworthy man in the jungle. He was brought up on an island at the mouth of the Essequibo and told us the worst thing that ever had happened to him was treading in the mud on a sting ray. Around his home he often found old Dutch gin bottles and he was kind enough to give us some to take home.

One evening he got talking. He told us some time ago he saw, after dark a skeleton slowly walking towards him. As it got closer it also talked to him. It turned out to be a man who had painted his body with florescent powder from a fungus or mushroom growing on rotten trees. I had seen that fungus on fallen trees. It crossed my mind that I could use it to "paint" the small clay figures I was making, the same way, the next time I saw it in the bush. Mr. Best also showed me how to shine a torch into the branches of trees to catch the eyes of animals which might be sitting above us.

Being away from the services of a barber I used to cut Nick's hair myself. The other men saw this and took advantage of my "services". Some of the men being of African descent had thick, curly hair which was a new experience for me. It was impossible to use a comb and I had just to cut straight into their hair. Well, they seemed to appreciate my work. It used to cost Nick a kiss, the other men got it for free.

One of my "costumers" was an African from just outside Georgetown called Yankee. He used to travel the jungles as a *pork knocker*. They would spend time away from civilisation searching for gold or diamonds. This name was given to them because of the pork provision they took with them. Pork trotters were imported from Europe, where they were not appreciated, and were skilfully used to produce delicious dishes locally. They became a national dish of Guyana. Sometimes the name *pork-barrel knocker* was used because pickled wild pork was kept in big barrels like the ones we had in our camp full of salted pork and which Palakia also enjoyed.

Many locals would try their luck going up the rivers to pan for gold. This involved a pan and water. When loaded with sand and mixed with water, the heavy parts would sink to the middle of the pan when it was vigoursly shaken and the lighter materials would rise to the top and be washed out by hand. Hopefully the heavy gold would then shine up at you, but most often nothing or just minute particles would be found, if it was a lucky day. It looked so easy, but it was difficult and hard to do efficiently. Most of the men said they had found small pieces of gold or maybe that was just what they would tell you! Of course no one would tell if they found a good spot in the jungle.

Another hair "customer" was an African from Georgetown by the name of George. He was deeply Christian and he spontaneously started to give services to the camp. He was very enthusiastic and gathered a small group especially on Sundays. As an example of his broad thinking, he asked me to say The Lord's prayer in Danish. I do not know how much people understood, but he felt he could follow the prayer.

Teaching Danish to George and Harold.

The Christian faith was often expressed in unusual and very Guyanese ways. I once saw painted on a boat "Prepare to meet thy God".

One day I was cutting Nick's hair as he was sitting on a chair and I tried to get his curls under control, when a British geologist, working in the jungle, suddenly and most unexpected stepped out of the bush. We were as surprised to see him as he was to see us. It turned out that our visitor was Jevan Berrangé from the BGS (British Geological Survey). We did not know each other before that day, but this first meeting was never forgotten and the beginning of a lifelong friendship.

He published in 2015 an account of his adventures travelling by canoe with Wai-Wai Amerindians in the far south of the country.

On the way to collect visitors

11. Survival and provisions

Almost everything we ate had to be brought into the camp. It could travel in by boat on the rivers and smaller creeks or it could be transported across land on rough tracks using the Survey's bombardier.

The bombardier transporting equipment and men arriving at Groete Creek camp with Mr. Best driving.

This vehicle can only be described as looking like the lower part of a tank complete with its tracks. It was always driven by Mr. Best. He had the bombardier completely under control. He kept it repaired and oiled. Sitting on top or just hanging on the sides when travelling through the bush, it often felt that we were heading straight into a tree, but this never happened. Just in the last minute, the bombardier would move to the side, avoiding the tree and set off in another direction towards the next tree.

This was a slow journey. People and provisions would be shaken around: it was so bumpy that one really had to hang on all the time, when moving through the undergrowth. But it was practical as any large things, such as drums of petrol, salted beef or pork in wooden drums and sacks of rice, could be carried, since this was all too heavy for the small boats. In an area with many waterfalls it was also an easier way of transport. But it did mean tracks and in some cases bridges had to be built.

It was lovely to have the drums of salted meat as they could keep for months. But there was another way of preserving meat which was a speciality that, as far as I know, is only used in Guyana. This was *cassareep*, which consists of a thick brown liquid made from bitter cassava roots with added jungle products such as roots, leaves and delicious spices. It was originally made by the Amerindians and its use later spread all over the country. It was invaluable in the jungle since cassava has antiseptic qualities and if the meat was boiled up just once every day, it would last forever, even in a hot climate. The taste was delicious with its slightly spicy undertones and it was used in a dish called *cassareep pepper pot*, another of the national dishes of Guyana.

Bitter cassava is a root that grows easily in jungle areas. The Amerindians harvest the roots and grate them. The juice contained within the raw root is poisonous as it contains cyanide. This is ingenuously extracted from the grated material using elongated tubes or *matapi* woven from vines collected in the forest. These were filled with grated cassava, hung from a beam and pulled downwards into a thin shape allowing the juice to be squeezed out. It would be interesting to know how this clever process was discovered. Presumably this was yet another accidental, bush discovery.

The grated cassava could also be used like flour for baking "flat bread" which would dry on the roofs of the Amerindian round houses. We broke the bread into smaller pieces and dipped into hot spicy sauce. It was delicious and I enjoyed it, when visiting Amerindian villages.

Matapies used for squeezing cyanide juice out of grated bitter cassava.

Baking cassava flat bread on a hot stone.

Drying cassava flat breads on a roof top.

Occasionally the men would fish and return with enormous catches to be enjoyed by us all. A small fish called Piranha was also present in most rivers, but was avoided wherever possible as it had jaws like a cat's being filled with vicious looking teeth. I was told they might attack at any time and that they could clean a man to a skeleton in minutes (this ability was once included in a James Bond film). When the big cattle ranches drove animals from the savannas in the south to Georgetown, they would let one steer go into the river first just in case. Then the herd could pass in relative safety. The danger for us was that was no one knew when and where they might be attacked and we all bathed in rivers in which they lurked.

A Piranha I caught with its cat-like teeth.

A vaquero with a Yakato fish from the Rupununi.

A tasty Haimara caught by Alvin in the Semarang River.

Sometimes we could run out of meat and then a hunter would go out with a shot gun for fresh provision. He would be given only one cartridge and told what kind of animal he should bring back. He always came back with our exact request. It might take three days to follow a Tapir or a bush cow as they are known in Guyana. Eventually when close, the hunter would see just one leaf moving and shoot. On one occasion, the Tapir was so big that half of it was left overnight after it was covered up to prevent it being eaten. Sometimes we might ask for the world's biggest rodent, the Capybara or an

Armadillo. We enjoyed eating everything the hunters could bring to supplement our otherwise simple diet. How they unerringly met our varied requests and never got lost in the process remains another complete mystery to us.

Early in the morning around five am a whiff of baking would begin to drift through the camp. Yeast and flour was also transported in for this purpose. The men built ovens from empty kerosene drums by placing them on their side and digging them half way into the ground. The drums were covered with fire, both on top and underneath them. The rising breads were placed on a shelf inside. Everyone would then be ready to go to work at seven armed with fresh bread. It was delicious and called colloquially *roti.*

At other times, they would prepare food directly over a bonfire or using a kerosene fuelled Primus for cooking. These looked easy to pump up and cook on. In reality, I found them very temperamental. One day Walter was unwell and I tried to make the primus work myself. After only managing to cover the camp with smoke, George took pity on me, or may be more practically to save everyone from the annoying smoke, and showed me how to do it. Well, we live and learn.

Mr. Best cutting up a 'bush cow' (Tapir).

When people went away to visit family or go to town, we would have a chance to order special provisions, even though it took some time before we received them. We could also send messages over the radio for provisions, which would wait for the next transport to come on the steamer to Bartica, from where it would be transported up river to our camp. If I had the opportunity to get some food, I would order rye bread, which is a healthier alternative to white bread, and which all Danes eat. Even at that time when living in London, it was only found in special departments. So what a surprise that in 1969 I could buy it in a local shop in Guyana! It appeared in round tins containing pumpernickel and was a wonderful supplement and a much appreciated change to my regular roti diet.

We were lucky to have oats for breakfast as well. However since there was no milk available many including Nick preferred to eat them not only raw but completely dry as well. To add some taste pepper or chilli was added on top. So there they were sitting in a dust cloud eating raw oats. I personally would have added water to make porridge, but each to their own.

The provision tent also contained egg powder. This seemed to be a relic from the wartime. Some people recognised it, but I had never heard of it. I tried to make pancakes using it on the primus stove, but I didn't seem to have the knack. It was very lumpy to work with and would not hang together. How did they manage during the war?

One time when passing several camps, it was obvious that something was brewing as bottles stood outside with foam coming out over the top. Out of curiosity I had to ask what was going on. Rice wine was being produced. Rice and sugar, when standing in the tropical heat for some time would ferment to produce a strong wine. Indeed too strong for me.

12. Travel between camps

Occasionally, when work had been completed in one area and the evidence indicated good resources somewhere else, the whole camp would move to a new location. Tarpaulins were rolled up and equipment placed in big trunks ready to be carried to the boat. Once loaded, we were ready to set off, either up or down the river. At other times, where there were tracks, the bombardier was used for very bulgy or heavy things, like drilling equipment.

Portaging on the Cuyuni River at Upper Kamaria.

A remaining problem was the birds that were rarely ever ready to be moved. Once when breaking camp, Palakia was far up a tree beyond climbing height and would not come when called. The solution was easy. The tree was quickly axed down and she was angrily delivered to us in a cloud of branches and leaves. Such action would be frowned on in these environmentally sensitive days, but there was no other choice as it might be hours before she chose to return.

Moving down the river one day the clouds looked ominous. Sitting on the side of the boat listening to the monotonous sound of the motors and the water, I began to feel sleepy. I moved to the middle of the boat and crept under the tarpaulin, covering all the equipment, where I found a trunk. Putting my arms on top and resting my head on it, I quickly fell asleep. When I woke up and appeared again from under the tarpaulin, it was getting dark and everyone around the sides of the boat looked very miserable and wet. Apparently an enormous thunderstorm had passed by and I was the only dry person on board. I had no idea, having heard nothing.

If the river was passable the journey was easy. Where there were falls, large fallen trees or boulders, the boat had to be emptied and everything had to be carried around the obstacle. After being placed back in the boat we could proceed. This was called *portaging*. It could happen several times in a day. But when the water way was high, we could run the rapids. This was exciting as sometimes we passed inland through the flooded bush at great speed.

Portaging the Arikunda Falls in the Semang River.

Emptied bateau riding the Arikunda Falls.

Portaging the Grass Falls in the Semang River.

Running the Tinamu Falls on the Cuyuni River with the two Captain Cramers in charge.

Sailing through the bush when the Cuyuni was in full flood

Captain Johnson running the flooded Cuyuni.

Captain Mosely hauling his boat around rapids.

A long length of the Cuyuni River just above Bartica is not passable by portaging due to the length of the rapids. A road was built to move boats around them and Mr. Rafferty provided the transport, though his vehicles were on the rough and ready side. But eventually we always somehow got across.

Mr Rafferty once offered us a ride in his NEW lorry. It looked like it had known better days with no glass in the windows. It was difficult to close the doors and as we started the door would not close, Mr. Rafferty in his annoyance resolutely pulled off the top of the door and threw it into the bush. We looked at each other and thought that soon there would be nothing left of his NEW truck.

Traffic jam in the wild.

Mr. Rafferty's NEW truck.

We had one big trunk just for kitchen utensils. At a temporary campsite, it was suggested that the camp attendant should only take those kitchen tools out of the trunk he would need for producing the meal for that evening. He protested and said that was not possible. Having listened to the discussion, I agreed with him. How many women would ahead of cooking know how many utensils they would use? You might need a spoon to this and a knife for that. It would be impossible for him to run up and down the riverside to collect what he needed. I supported him and then grudgingly the heavy kitchen trunk was carried off the boat and into the kitchen tent. For him it was easier to have everything at hand and to pack it down quickly again.

On another occasion he was in trouble for making too much rustling noise with an aluminium space blanket we had given him. Camp attendants I found out, had a funny position in the camp hierarchy lying somewhere between those of the geologists and the others.

One day we again had to proceed to another camp. I stepped down into a smaller boat with my bag over my shoulder, but I lost my balance and in that moment my reflex was to swing my arm right up in the air to keep my balance. My bag flew away and made a huge circle in the air and now could be seen floating away down the river, together with papers and its other contents which were spreading out over a big area in the water. Again thanks to the competence of the men, everything was saved from the water by their quick action.

Some boats were easy to climb into, but others could be quite small. Trying to paddle a "dug out" was quite and experience Every movement of the muscles make the trunk twitch. By the time I had my muscles under control, the trunk had taken its own course down the river. Only after some time did I manage to control the movements and paddle it in the right direction. The men of course had done this sort of thing all their lives and found it hilarious that I could not control the dugout.

Learning to paddle a dugout during a visit to a village.

When on the river I occasionally had to take action. One day the water was seeping in faster than we could bail it out of the boat. It was easy to see where the leak was. I therefore took some old cloth and with a knife put it in between the leaking planks. It worked well and for the rest of the journey we only had to bail water now and again.

13. Unusual happenings during usual work

As mentioned before, the capacity to know in what directions to walk through the jungle is invaluable. The men had no problem with this. I often realised just how easy it was to lose the way. As soon as one is surrounded by the bush and there is no cut path, it is easy to walk in a circle and get nowhere. Having read about other people's survival, the safest way when lost, is to find and follow a river or creek, as at least this will prevent walking forever in circles. Also a river might arrive at a village, lumber camp or the coast. But rivers are not always straight forward to follow and the distances might be immense. However, there would always be water to drink.

Occasionally the men let me lead the walk through the forest. They were just testing me on how well I would manage on my own. I imagined I could see where other people had troth a path. The leaves on the ground seemed more compact. I soon learned that the men looked out on existing path as to where a cutlass had been used to cut the branches to open a path. In thin jungle these cuts might be few and far between and care was needed. But that was a safer strategy than looking on the ground.

Brown river and sunlight.

On such trips animals were often observed. They were pointed out to me and even when I tried to look in the right direction, I could never see anything. Many times the men saw big cats or tapirs, but rarely did I have the skills to notice anything other than trees.

Digging test pits. The possibility of building a dam across the Cuyuni was being investigated. As far as I know nothing resulted from so much hard work.
Jerry Jarvis, Michael and Joe, with Richard in the hole.

The men sometimes had to walk into rivers finding that way easier than going through tangled bush. They would tie rope around their trouser legs to prevent ticks crawling up. It is possible to return to camp and having to get rid of quite a number gorging themselves on your blood. These were mainly on the legs, but they could be anywhere on the body, often in inconvenient and tender places.

When removing leeches, it is important to detach the mouth pieces. The best way to achieve this was to use a match and burn them until they let go. This minimised the risk of them leaving mouth pieces in the skin which could later cause infections. But this was not always easy to do without burning oneself in the process.

Another risk of walking for long hours in the water or being constantly wet is getting fungus infections, especially between the toes. This can be a severe problem in hot moist climates making walking difficult and leading to sores and infections. We had no treatment, but I found that using iodine got rid of the infections. I had that with me for treating minor cuts anyway.

When walking through the bush, I had often had to climb over fallen trees. Such actions when repeated many times throughout the day was awfully tiring. At other times when going down steep hills, a normal reaction is to catch hold of trees to stop sliding down. In this situation it was important to see where ones hands were placed since many trees are covered, for protection with big, sharp thorns. In the moment of imbalance, it is only too easy just to grasp the nearest tree: getting rid of the thorns later could be tricky. Another risk at such times is disturbing bees, wasps or hornets whilst concentrating on the ground ahead and where to place my feet.

When a tree falls across a small river or gully it becomes a useful bridge. These natural bridges are called a *takuba*. Unfortunately, their rough surfaces can be slippery to walk on, especially just after rain. When I had to cross takubas someone kindly gave me a stick to keep my balance to prevent me falling off.

At one time we had to walk to another camp. The men went ahead carrying heavy loads. I followed behind. We had to cross a takuba, this time lying across a deep gully. I slowly started to walk out. Then in the middle I suddenly panicked and froze. I realised that I was alone and could not attract anyone's attention. I could not look down. It felt like I was standing there forever. I concentrated on looking at the wood of the takuba in front of me and eventually steeled myself to continue by carefully moving foot by foot forward, so slowly, slowly. Miraculously I reached the other side. That was the worst and most dangerous incident in all the time I spent in the bush.

Sylvin Ferreira using a takuba to cross a gully.

One day Nick and I had gone for a walk when we suddenly heard a running noise from the bush. He said it sounded like a herd of wild pigs. They are often aggressive and would attack. Hunters, I was told, would always shoot the last one in the herd as this would not alert the others. Here we were and what to do? Fortunately a takuba was nearby. We crawled out to sit in the middle, back to back. I expect if anyone had seen us, it would have looked comical, but there was no one anywhere nearby. Luckily we did not have to fight them off with our sticks as they were just running past. Throughout we never actually saw any pigs.

One day a camp member returned from Georgetown telling us of a devastating happening. The Governor General of Guyana, Sir David Rose, had been killed during a visit to London. The men were numbed. They just stood around hardly talking. I shall never forget the date: November the 10th 1969. Some scaffolding had fallen down and killed him, near Whitehall. It was shocking. I remember one of the men's comments was "typical English behaviour!"

During a traverse in the bush, a visiting geologist happened to stand under a tree with a howling monkey unknowing to him squatting above. For some reason it began to howl. Their howls are excessively loud and scary, and the geologist lost his notes and was quite shaken. Not surprisingly, the howling monkeys can be heard over the treetops from far away. It is a most incredible noise that just grows and grows in crescendo. How unfortunate to stand just under one about to howl.

There is nothing like waking up in the morning, sticking your feet out of the hammock and realising that the camp is under water. Everything was floating around. Instead of walking through the camp, the communication was now by boat. Each time we needed to collect things or talk to somebody, shouting was necessary for accessing transport. However the flood would not last longer than one could spend the time on top of the table or in the hammock. At least I could reach my beloved book shelf.

Flooded camp after a storm.

The bush is full of strange and sometimes loud noises. For days I could hear whining, sharp, complaining, and crying out noises. It sounded different from that of howling monkeys. It turned out to be a hollow tree which the wind, when in a certain direction, would blow through a hole and create a noise. It could be heard from far away. Sometimes this phenomenon was useful for deciding on a meeting point as everyone would know the tree in question and thus where to go. Some people thought of it as a ghost. One Amerindian, Arthur Ready from Saxacalli, told Nick that it was a spirit calling out in distress. He had a name for it .There always seemed to be many stories to explain such strange phenomena.

14. How I used my time

Each night my husband briefed the camp's foreman on the coming day's work who would then allocate men for each task. Often I would join work parties from the camp when my accompanying them was compatible with the activities being done that day. I always learned something on these occasions. At other times, I used the time well in the camp site. Apart from reading, I also had embroidery to finish off. I sat in a clearing just at the edge of the camp where the sun shone. My fear was to lose the needle. But quite another problem was the humidity. The needle would rust. I now have a finished, embroidered map of Denmark hanging on the wall with a rust mark in the linen where I left the needle after finishing the work.

The Sand Creek crew with Nick in the background.

I started all sorts of other activities whenever I could. For example, there was plenty of mud around and I began to make small figures of clay. My favourite was a small mouse sitting with its nose in the air and which had a tail and whiskers made of tiny roots stuck into the clay. The figures dried nicely in the sun so I did not need to ask to have them "fired" in the big bread baking drums.

My attempts to seed carrots and other vegetables were a disaster. The ants liked the seeds and maybe they were unsuitable for the tropical climate anyway. But I was successful with an Amarillo lily which I planted in a sunny place. It flowered with a most beautiful, red colour and was a spectacular and unusual sight in the middle of all the greenery. It was doubly enjoyable since we never saw the flowers at the top of the trees, but only realised that they existed higher up, when seeing the petals below on the ground, either naturally falling or attacked by our birds,

I had brought my guitar with me and for once learned all my lessons because I had plenty of time for practice. It must have been strange for a passing visitor to suddenly to hear a guitar under the canopy. The men also had a go and were very clever when playing. We had much enjoyment. They also liked to be photographed with the guitar, even though they were maybe not yet able to play.

Philbert and Tony James strumming. Walter looking like a real troubadour.

Suddenly, someone provided shuttle cocks and rackets. Guyanese are eminent badminton players, and because they followed the Olympics, they knew all the Danish players. They thought that I would know all the players privately, but even though they were famous, that was not the case. The men quickly realised that my playing was not up to Olympic standards. We had no net, but that was not a problem as a rope could be used. We spend quite some time hitting scuttle cocks to and fro.

Playing badminton with Walter.

To pass time, one of the men had been drawing me. He was very clever and I was surprised to be given his drawings. I still have them in my Guyana album.

Raphael's drawing of me playing the guitar

Another of Raphael's drawings, this time with Palakia on my knee..

15. What we did next

Travelling around on the rivers or when in Georgetown or Bartica we sometimes met people who invited us to join them where they lived and worked in the interior. We also had invitations to visit the homes and villages of men who were working for Nick.

One of those people we met was a priest who also had farming knowledge. He used this experience to improve the diet of his parishioners who were Akawaio Amerindians living high up the Mazaruni River. As no one spoke English, he had to learn the language and understand the local culture. One of his farming ideas to improve living conditions was to add pigs to the hens which were already pecking around in the village. Getting them there was not easy. On one occasion, he took a pig with him on a plane and registered it as hand baggage for the flight from Georgetown to the interior. During the journey the pig was sick and the owner was reminded that his hand baggage was moving around and was severely airsick. This story shows how thinking outside the box is necessary to solve problems in this environment.

In front of an Amerindian house in the Rupununi with Roger Varu on my shoulder.

In the village, though people had great knowledge and experience, superstition was also rife. For example, at night time it was believed that bad spirits moved around and that they would punish anyone who had behaved wrongly. They would describe the spirits they saw as taking the form of animals. Looking back was this in reality a clever way of the village chief or shaman of controlling people who misbehave in society? It was also believed that some people had powers to make others sick. One of the chiefs, it was said, had "blown" on the priest, for an unknown reason. But the priest, who did not believe this, had to confess that he had a stiff neck for a while.

In this village we spent several days enjoying the hospitality of the priest and his wife. We were swimming in the river with their three daughters and the wife provided splendid food for us even though the possibilities of provisions were limited. I was amazed by her ingenuity and she told me how precious a simple thing like an egg was.

Akawaio Amerindians with bows and arrows and carrying cassava and fire wood.

On another occasion we visited the savannahs of the Rupununi. It was here that he big cattle ranches were located. The ranch we visited was called Dadanawa. It was written about in 1956 by Edwina Melville who described the ranch and its surroundings. We had the luck to spend some days here being able to ride out with the local people, the *vaqueros*, to find escaped cows and repair fences. I am not a good rider and the small horse I was given was not too eager to go faster than a walk. But as soon as a vaquero was sitting on it, it could really move. They used small narrow stirrups so they could ride barefoot.

Walking on the savannah at Orinduik with Roger Varu.
A young Amerindian girl took this picture using my camera.

One day we were driving across the savannah in a Land Rover when we saw another vehicle coming towards us. It is so rare to meet other people here so of course we stopped to talk. Two men were driving a Mini Moke, an open sided vehicle ideal for the tropical heat. Its sole disadvantage was that all sorts of flies and biting insects were swept in with the cooling air. The usual questions of where are you from revealed that they were British and it turned out they were from the same area where we lived. One of them, Douglas McMinn, was the owner of a building supplies company who had donated much to improve the conditions of elderly people in his home town of Chesham (his centre is still there today). It is a small world we live in.

During the evening we would go down to the river. But here the worst of insects would suddenly swarm all over us. These were small biting sand flies called locally a *pium*. They left an incredible itching and I would scratch the bites for days. I have photos with marks all over arms and legs. Fortunately, these only struck when you went down to a river.

At another time, forever exploring, we found ourselves travelling across the savannahs again. This time we were in the company with some people from Trinidad. That evening we invited the chief from the nearby village to dinner. After having unpacked in the hut we were offered, we saw to our surprise that the whole village was arriving for supper. The contingent included entire families and the total number arriving was some fifty people. The only solution was to open all our provisions and pour them all into the biggest pot we would find. The mixture included soups, vegetables and tinned meat, we just opened everything. To serve it we gave each family half of a lunchbox as a bowl, plus a spoon to share. Everyone seemed to enjoy the evening. Surprisingly enough, it was remarkably tasty. Ever since this experience, I have not been worried about mixing all kinds of food together.

Akawaio boy in a hammock.

After coming out of the bush and returning to Georgetown we took part in local activities. We attended festivals such as Diwali, the festival of lights, and Holi when everyone is covered by accident and design in brightly coloured powders. The tradition in Guyana is to drink rum at parties. During one of the parties when the rum bottles were brought out we noticed that the pictures on the walls of the Hindu gods were covered up with tea towels, since the house owners did not want the gods to see us drinking.

On Independence Day everyone danced or "tramped" in the streets following behind a lorry carrying a steel band. In this way big crowds would enjoy themselves until late into the night. On the 23.February 1970 when Guyana became a republic, we took part in the atmosphere and gaiety dancing our way around the city. I especially loved the steel bands and whenever I hear their sound, it brings me back to Guyana.

Epilogue

I have learned with sadness that the bush expeditions I so much enjoyed are no longer routinely taking place. I will always miss the jungle, the atmosphere, the camaraderie, the rivers, the animals and insects, the sun when it appeared between the trees, and even the thunder and rain.

We have memories of our time in Guyana in our home: several animals carved in wood, baskets of woven vines, warishees, teeth from a Piranha and a blowpipe standing in a corner. Since we also have several poisoned darts for the blowpipe, I have practiced using it by blowing darts into sofa cushions. It is amazing how accurate they are with just a sight made of two Agouti teeth fixed on top of the pipe. No sound is heard, which is why the Amerindians are able to be so effective in their hunting. When shooting parrots this silence enabled them to hit many birds before they would notice and fly away. I found out later that the pipe is produced by letting sand run through the hollow middle of the tube. What patience it takes to make a good blowpipe.

One of the things I missed most in the bush was fresh fruit. Because I had taken some limes with me, I planted the pips after having used the juice. I scattered them around the camp protecting them in the ground. I like to think that some seeds survived the attentions of the ants, the scratching of animals and the erosion of the soil caused by the heavy downpours.

Perhaps passing travellers will have enjoyed encountering a lime tree or two in the middle of nowhere and will have used the fruits to sustain them as they travelled along the river, just as I did so many years ago.